LOOK AGAIN

SENIOR AUTHORS

Virginia A. Arnold   **Carl B. Smith**

AUTHORS

James Flood   **Diane Lapp**

LITERATURE CONSULTANTS

Joan I. Glazer   Margaret H. Lippert

Macmillan/McGraw-Hill School Publishing Company
New York   Chicago   Columbus

Macmillan/McGraw-Hill School Division
866 Third Avenue
New York, New York 10022

Printed in the United States of America

ISBN 0-02-178716-6

9 8 7 6 5 4 3 2

ACKNOWLEDGMENTS

The publisher gratefully acknowledges permission to reprint the following copyrighted material:

"Keep a Poem in Your Pocket" by Beatrice Schenk de Regniers. Copyright © 1958, 1986 by Beatrice Schenk de Regniers. Reprinted by permission of the author.

"Little" from EVERYTHING AND ANYTHING by Dorothy Aldis. Copyright © 1925–1927, copyright renewed 1953–1955 by Dorothy Aldis. Reprinted by permission of G.P. Putnam's Sons.

"My Mama Needs Me" is the entire text of MY MAMA NEEDS ME by Mildred Pitts Walter. Text copyright © 1983 by Mildred Pitts Walter. Illustrations by Pat Cummings. Illustrations copyright © 1983 by Pat Cummings. Adapted by permission of Lothrop, Lee & Shepard Books (A Division of William Morrow & Company). Used by permission also of McIntosh & Otis, Inc.

"The River Is a Piece of Sky" from THE REASON FOR THE PELICAN by John Ciardi. Copyright © 1959 by John Ciardi. Used by permission of the author.

"The Secret" adapted from AMANDA PIG AND HER BIG BROTHER OLIVER by Jean Van Leeuwen. Text copyright © 1980 by Jean Van Leeuwen. Illustrations copyright © 1980 by Ann Schweninger. Reprinted by permission of the publisher, Dial Books for Young Readers. Also by permission of Sheldon Fogelman for the author.

"Teach Us, Amelia Bedelia" is the entire text of TEACH US, AMELIA BEDELIA by Peggy Parish. Text copyright © 1977 by Margaret Parish. Illustrations by Lynn Sweat. Illustrations copyright © 1977 by Lynn Sweat. Abridged by permission of Greenwillow Books (A Division of William Morrow & Company). By permission also of World's Work Ltd.

"Tito Perez" is from the book POEMAS PARVULOS by Ernesto Galarza where it begins with the words "Pito Perez…" Used by permission.

"Who's in Rabbit's House?" is a dramatization of WHO'S IN RABBIT'S HOUSE? by Verna Aardema. Text copyright © 1969, 1977 by Verna Aardema. Reprinted by permission of Curtis Brown, Ltd. Illustrations by Leo and Diane Dillon copyright © 1977. Used by permission of the publisher, Dial Books for Young Readers and Sheldon Fogelman.

Cover Design: Josie Yee
Feature Logos and Medallion Logos: Eva Vagreti Cockrille
Unit Openers: Bob Shein

ILLUSTRATION CREDITS: Sal Murdocca, 4–8; Marie Louise-Gay, 18–24; Jan Jones, 27, 88–89, 148, 158–159, 182–183; Ann Schweninger, 28–35; Susan Dodge, 38–48; Bernadette Lau, 50–59; Jan Pyk, 61, 199; Mac Evans, 62–63; Jerry Smath, 64–75; Stephen Perringer, 76–77; Fernando Fernandez, 78–87; Tim Hildebrandt, 100–111; Linda Strauss-Edwards, 114–121; Volker Theinhardt, 122–123; Pat Cummings, 134–145; Lynn Titleman, 146–147; Richard Steadham, 160–171; Daryl Moore, 172–181; Leo & Diane Dillon, 184–197; Lynn Sweat, 200–215; Gala Godell, 217–236; Lane Yerkes, 242–255.

PHOTO CREDITS: ANIMALS ANIMALS: 150T; © Margo Conte, 155T; © John Cooke, 92CR; © E.R. Degginger, 152BL, 156TR; © David C. Fritts, 153TR; © Patti Murray, 91L; Oxford Scientific Films, 93; © Souricat, 94B. © Walter Chandoha, 92B. BRUCE COLEMAN, INC.: © Jen & Des Bartlett, 150B, 151CB, 152C; © Rod Borland, 94TL, © Jack W. Dykinga, 95B; © Jeff Foott, 153L; © Keith Gunnar, 95T; © C. Haagner, 156B; © M.P. Kahl, 155C; © Laura Riley, 156C; © G. Schaller, 155B; © Jamie Tanaka, 92T; © Norman Owen Tomalin, 92CL; © Jonathan Wright, 95 inset. DRK PHOTO: © Tom Bledsoe, 151T; © Jim Brandenburg, 152BR; © Johnny Johnson, 152T; © George J. Sanker, 153BR. © Ken Lax, 96. MAGNUM PHOTOS, INC.: © Burt Glinn, 154. © David L. Perry, 90, 97L. PHOTO RESEARCHERS, INC.: © Robert Carlyle Day, 97R; © Russ Kinne, 91R; © Tom McHugh, 94TR; © Simon, 93 inset. © Suzanne Szasz, 10 to 17, 124 to 131. WOODFIN CAMP & ASSOCIATES: © John Blaustein, 151CT; © Michal Heron, 151B.

Contents

4

5

8

FEELING GOOD

UNIT

1

We learn about our world with our five senses. We can see, hear, taste, smell, and touch. In this unit, you will read about the five senses. How do your senses help you?

The world is so full of a number of things,
I'm sure we should all be as happy as kings.

Robert Louis Stevenson

MY FIVE SENSES

Judith Davis

How do you find out things you want
to know?
You have five senses to help you.
Read to find out what your five senses
are, and how they help you.

I have five senses to help me do
things every day.
No matter where I go, they
help me know things
I want to know.

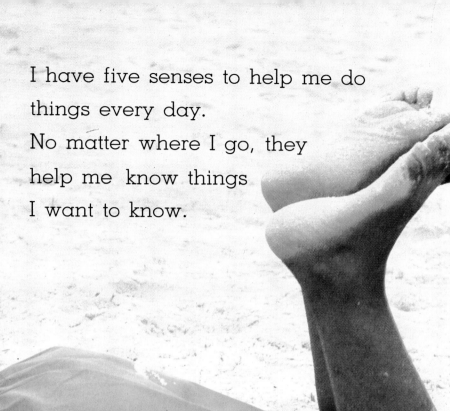

I see with my eyes.
I hear with my ears.
I smell with my nose.
I taste with my tongue.
I touch with my skin.

With my eyes, I can see where I go when I run into the water.

Jerry and I look for shells.

We watch the boats come and go, and we look out for fish.

I like to play water tag with Jerry.

It's fun to see the look on his face when I tag him!

Jerry dives down and shows me how to swim under the water.

With my ears, I hear the water.
I hear the birds up in the sky, too.
Jerry can hear the wind in pine trees.
He says he hears the wind make
little songs.

With my nose, I smell things.
There are things that smell good to me,
and things that don't smell so good.
When the tide is out, I don't like the
smell of the fish.

I do like the smell of flowers, and the
smell of a hot dog.
But more than anything, I like the smell
of the water.
What a good smell that is!
You will never find it in the city.

My sense of taste is a little like my sense
of smell.
There are things that taste good to me,
and things that don't taste so good.
I like the taste of water, but not the taste
of water I swim in!
I like the taste of the water I drink at home.

With my sense of touch, I get to know
things better.
It's like seeing with my skin.
Shells feel good in my hand, and the hot
sun feels good on my skin.
My sense of touch helps me.
I can feel when things are too hot
to touch.

I need my five senses every day,

no matter what I do.

I see, I hear, I smell, I taste, and I touch.

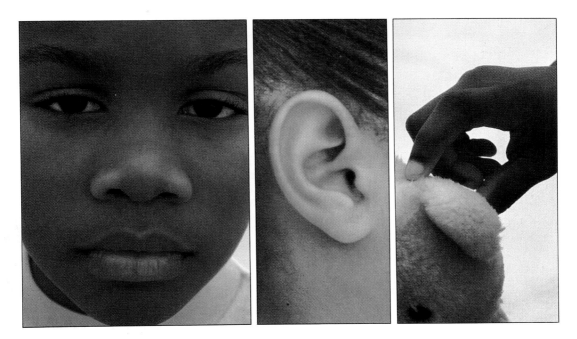

Thinking and Writing About the Selection

1. What do the five senses help this boy and girl to know?

2. What are the songs that Jerry says he can hear?

3. What do your senses help you know on a day in the city?

The Pet Frog

Dorothy Van Woerkom

Jack shows his new pet frog to his
friends Cindy and Bill.
Will the frog stay with Jack?
When you read, see how her sense of touch
helps Cindy get to know what a
frog is like.

18

Jack came to see Cindy and Bill.

"Do you want to see my new pet?" he asked.

He put a big green frog down on the floor.

19

"A frog!" Cindy said.
"Can a frog live out of the water?"

"It came out of the pond," said Jack.
"I will let it live there, but it's
my pet."

"What do you feed your frog?" Bill asked.

"It likes bugs," Jack said.

Cindy made a face and said, "It's silly
to like bugs."

"Not for a frog," said Jack.

Cindy put out her hand to take the frog.
"Will you come to me?" she asked, but the
frog did not come.
She picked up the frog and sat it on
her hand.
Then she laughed and said,
"It feels like ice!

Here, Bill, do you want to touch it?"

Bill looked at the frog.

"No," he said.

"I don't want to touch it, but I do want
to see it get a bug.
How soon will your frog want to have a
bug, Jack?"

"It may want a bug now," Jack said.

Cindy laughed.
"There are no bugs in here," she said,
"but I have a plan.
Come on!"
Cindy ran outside with the frog.

"Why did she take my frog?" asked Jack.

"I don't know why," Bill said.
"Cindy just likes to plan things."

Soon Cindy cried, "Come out and watch your frog get a fly, Jack!"

The boys ran outside.
Cindy and the frog were next to the pond, watching a big fly.
"What are you doing, Cindy?" asked Jack.
"What is your plan?"

"I will tell you my plan," said Cindy.
"You don't have to find bugs for your frog.
It will find its own.
I thought it could find a fly here, and I
was right.
Look!"

The boys looked, and out came the
frog's tongue.
Then there was no fly!

24

"Did you see that?" asked Bill.

Quickly the frog jumped into the water.

Cindy laughed and said, "Jack, that frog is not your pet, and I can tell you why."

"Why?" asked Jack.

"A pet likes to stay with you," said Cindy.
"That frog likes to stay in his own home—the pond!
You may want a pet frog, Jack, but that frog doesn't want you!"

Thinking and Writing About the Selection

1. What is it like to touch a frog?

2. How can a frog get a fly?

3. Why is the frog not a good pet for Jack?

SKILLS activity

FOLLOW DIRECTIONS

A. Read the words. Then follow the directions.

The Five Senses	Parts of the Body
to see	tongue
to hear	nose
to smell	skin
to taste	eyes
to touch	ears

1. Write the five senses on your paper.

2. After each sense write the part of the body that goes with it.

3. Find the sense that fits in each sentence. Write the sentences on your paper.

I _____ the hot dog with my tongue.

I _____ the boats with my eyes.

I _____ the sand with my skin.

I _____ the birds with my ears.

I _____ the flower with my nose.

B. How can you find out about feeding a pet?

You can read the directions in a book.

How to Feed Your Fish

• Feed your fish one time a day.
• Each fish gets one bit.

Now answer the questions.

1. When do you feed the fish?

2. Does each fish get two bits?

bird   cat   fish   fox   frog

lion   pony   seal   dog   snake

C. What animal will make a good pet?

Look at the pictures.

Then follow the directions.

1. Write the names of all the animals on your paper.

2. Circle the names of animals that live in the water.

3. Underline the names of animals that make good pets.

27

THE SECRET

Jean Van Leeuwen   Illustrated by Ann Schweninger

The sense of touch helps Mother,
Oliver, and Amanda have a good hug.
Read to find out what sense helps them
play a game.

It was raining outside.

Mother and Oliver and Amanda were
in the big chair, having a hug.

"Tell me a secret," said Oliver.

"All right," said Mother.

Mother whispered a secret into
Oliver's ear.
"We are as snug as three bugs in
a rug," she said.

"Me too," said Amanda.

"First I have to tell my tiger,"
said Oliver.
Oliver whispered the secret into his
tiger's ear.
"Three bugs are having a hug,"
he said.

"Now me," said Amanda.

Oliver's tiger whispered the secret into
Amanda's ear.
"Three bugs are on the rug," he said.

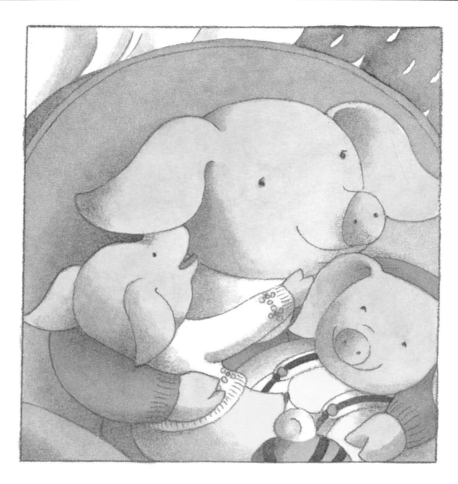

"Can you tell me,
Amanda?" asked Mother.

Amanda whispered the secret into
Mother's ear.
"Bug in your ear," she said.

"What bug?" cried Mother.

"Where?"

Mother jumped up and slapped her ear.

Oliver and Amanda fell on the floor.

Mother fell on top of them.

"Oh, my," said Mother.

She sat up.

"Where did the bug go?" she asked.

"There was no bug," said Oliver.

"It was just a secret."

Mother laughed.

Oliver and Amanda laughed.

They laughed and laughed.

And the three of them had another
big hug on the rug.

Thinking and Writing About the Selection

1. At first, where are Mother, Oliver,
   and Amanda having a hug?

2. How did Mother, Oliver, and Amanda
   get to the rug?

3. How did the secret change?

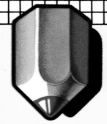

WRITING activity

WORD PICTURE

Prewrite

In the story, "The Pet Frog," Cindy
picks up Jack's frog and says,
"It feels like ice."
That is a good word picture.
You can tell how a frog feels when you
read that sentence.
Your five senses can help you write word pictures.

With the help of his five senses, Jack
thought of sentences to write for a word
picture for his pet frog.

SENSE	SENTENCE
SEE	My little frog is gray-green.
SEE	He hops high as the moon on legs.
TOUCH	His skin feels like ice.
HEAR	"Ribbit, ribbit," he says to me.
SMELL	My pet can smell just like the woods when it's raining.
TASTE	My frog likes the taste of a fly on his tongue.

Write

1. Write a word picture of your pet or a pet you wish you could have.
2. First, think of the pet.
   Let your five senses help you plan sentences for your word picture.
3. Now, write your first sentence.
   You may want to say:
   My pet is a ——————.
4. Then write sentences that tell what your pet is like.

Revise

1. Read your word picture.
   Have a friend read it, too.
2. Think of these things as you read.
   Do your sentences tell just what your pet is like?
   Did you put all five senses in your word picture?
   What words could you change in your sentences to make a better word picture?

Louise

Ada Litchfield

Louise doesn't have five senses.
She is blind.
Read to find out how her sense of
touch helps her to "see" things.

My name is Louise and I am blind.
This is my mother, my father, my
grandmother, my dog Leo, and
my good friend Ben.

Ben and I have fun all the time.
He likes a good joke, and so do I.
He likes to make up songs, and so do I.
He likes to play tricks on me, but I
don't mind.
I play tricks on him, too.

It makes me happy to go for walks with Ben.
One time he picked up a frog, and
he let me touch it.
That's how I know how things look.
I touch them.

When we go to the lake to swim, my
grandmother likes to come, too.
She likes to swim.
I still don't know how to swim, but my
grandmother says it will make her happy
to show me how.
That's my grandmother.
She's my good friend, and I like to make
her happy.

Do I mind not seeing?

Yes, I do.

But with the help of my family, my friend
Ben, and my cane, I can do things.

I need my cane.

It helps me walk.

If I have my cane, I know I won't walk
into things.

If I have my cane, I know where to walk.

When we were having a play at school, I
asked Ben for his help.
"What is the name of the play?" Ben asked.

"It's a secret," I said.

"Who are you in the play?" asked Ben.

"It's a secret," I said again.

"What can I do to help?" asked Ben.
"Is that a secret, too?"

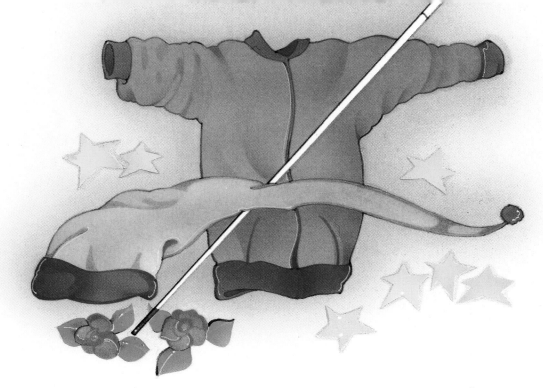

"First, please get the red flowers out of
this bag," I said to Ben, and he did.

"I have all the red flowers," said Ben.
"Now what?"

"Now, please keep my cane still," I said,
"and I will glue the flowers on it."
Next I asked Ben to make stars for me.

"Where will you put the stars?" asked Ben.
"Wait and you will see, Ben," I said.
Ben waited, and I got my coat and hat.

We put stars on my coat and hat for the
play, but then we got silly.
We put stars on the floor, and we put
stars on the chair legs.
Ben put stars on his legs, and I put
stars on my legs.
We laughed and laughed.

"I hope your mother doesn't mind,"
Ben said.

"She won't," I said.
"The stars and the glue will come off,
and she likes to get silly, too!"
We laughed again.

Then Ben said, "Show me your play," so I
got it out.
"Here it is," I said to him.

"I can't read this," he said.
"It's in Braille."

"Feel it, silly," I said, and he did.

"I still don't know what it says.
I can't read Braille," he said.

"You don't have to," I said.
"Just wait.
You will hear what it says when you
come to my school to see the play."

Then I put on my hat and coat.

I touched Ben with the cane and asked,

"Who am I?"

"I don't know," Ben said.

I could tell that he was a little mad.

"I look like a pretty grandmother," I said.

"I will help a girl get her wish.

She will go to a ball.

A man will see her there and . . ."

"I know, I know!" said Ben, and he jumped up and down.

Ben did know.

He said the name of the play.

He said who I was.

Do you know?

Thinking and Writing About the Selection

1. Who and what helps Louise do things?

2. What is Braille?

3. What do Ben and Louise do with the stars?

A FOOD SALE

Argentina Palacios

Lupita and Charito help with a
food sale at school.
What food will they make for the sale?
As you read, watch for the senses of
taste and smell.

"Boys and girls," said Mr. Raymond, "tell your mother and father that we will take a school trip in the spring.
We will go to Mexico.
They will have to come to school and see me if you want to come along."

Lupita and Charito couldn't wait to tell Mama!

"What is it, girls?" Mama asked when
they got home.

"Mama, may we go to Mexico in the
spring?" asked Lupita.

"You have to go to see Mr. Raymond, if we
can go," said Charito.

"A trip to Mexico!" said Mama.
"What fun for you!
I will go and see Mr. Raymond.
Now, go tell your grandmother.
It will make her happy, because her home
was in Mexico when she was a girl.
We went there on a trip when I
was little."

The next day Mama went with the girls to
school to see Mr. Raymond.
She looked at the plan for the trip and
said that Lupita and Charito could go along.

Mr. Raymond said, "We need a bus for the trip, so we want to have a food sale."

"Who will make the food?" asked Lupita. "The boys and girls will make the food for the sale," said Mr. Raymond.

"What can we make?" asked Charito.

"That is up to you," said Mr. Raymond.

Lupita and Charito thought and thought of things they could make for the food sale. Then one day Grandmother said, "Why don't you make tacos?
I will show you the way to make them."

"Tacos smell good and taste good," said Lupita.

"They look so pretty, too!" said Charito.

54

On the day of the sale, the girls went
with Dad to get the things to make
the tacos.
When they got home Grandmother said, "I
will make the shells and your mother will
mix the beef."

Then Mama said to Lupita and Charito,
"You can put the beef in the shells, and
the things that go on top of the beef."

When they had made all the tacos they
wanted, Mama said, "Mmmm, the tacos
smell so good!
I want to eat one!"

"Mama!" said Lupita, "the tacos are for
the sale!"

"Just a taste?" asked Mama.

"Just one little taste, Mama," said Charito, and they all laughed.

Dad put the tacos in the car. Then the family went to the gym for the sale.

There was so much food for sale at the gym!
It was quite a show of tastes and smells.
"I will eat fish," said Dad.

"Beef with nuts!" said Mama.
"That looks very good."

"Who's having a hot dog?" asked Dad.

"I am!" cried Lupita and Charito at the
same time.

"There is Mr. Raymond!" said Mama.
First Mr. Raymond went one way,
then another.

"Do you like the food, Mr. Raymond?"
asked Lupita.

Mr. Raymond laughed and said, "I don't know what to eat first.
I wish I could eat all of it, but there is too much!
I know!
I will eat tacos first, because this food sale is for a trip to Mexico, and we will eat tacos there!"

"That makes me feel so good!" cried Charito, and they all laughed.

Thinking and Writing About the Selection

1. Why was there a food sale at the school?

2. How do you make tacos?

3. Why did Charito and Lupita want to go to Mexico?

ARGENTINA PALACIOS

"I always liked languages," Argentina Palacios recalls. Her grandfather was a writer and teacher, as is her mother. "So it seemed natural for me to follow their path." In fifth grade, Palacios wrote a prize-winning essay that was published in a newspaper in Panama, the country where she grew up.

Today she writes stories in both English and Spanish. "I get ideas from anything I read, hear, or see, and sometimes I use events from my own background. When I write a story, I'm not always sure what will happen. Sometimes it creates itself!"

More to Read   *The Knight and the Squire*
This Can Lick a Lollipop/Esto Goza

WHAT'S FOR DINNER?

GARDEN SALAD

Lettuce, beans, peppers, carrots, tomatoes

BEEF WITH NUTS

Beef and nuts on noodles

PIZZA

Pizza with cheese tomato sauce, mushrooms

SUSHI

Fish and rice wrapped in seaweed

TACO

Beef, cheese, lettuce, tomato in a taco shell

Here are good things to eat for dinner.

What foods do you think answer the questions?

1. What food is eaten in a shell?
2. What food has rice in the middle?
3. What food is eaten with noodles?
4. What foods come with cheese?

What foods do you like best?

Tito Pérez

Tito Pérez
¿de dónde eres?
Soy de Tonalá.
Tito Pérez,
¿dónde vives?
Vivo con mamá.
Dime, Tito,
muy quedito
¿qué haces en tu casa?
Hago quesos
muy sabrosos
con sal y mostaza.

Ernesto Galarza

62

Tito Pérez

Tito Pérez
Where are you from?
I'm from Tonala.
Tito Pérez
Where is your home?
I live with my mom.
Tell me, Tito,
Very softly,
What do you do at home?
I make cheese,
Such tasty cheese,
With salt and mustard
seed.

Ernesto Galarza

63

Look Again, Little Mouse

Jerry Smath

Every day you may see new things,
but watch out!
Your eyes may play tricks on you.
Little Mouse will soon find out that
not all things are what they look like.

At last spring had come to the woods.
Plants and trees were green again.
Every animal came out of its secret home.
All the animals wanted to see and touch
all that was new.

Little Mouse came out, too.
This was his first spring in the woods.
He ran from one flower to another, and
he touched every flower as he ran.
"I have never seen anything so pretty,"
he said.

65

Toad could see how happy Little Mouse was.
"The flowers are pretty," he said to
Little Mouse, "but not all things are
what they look like.
Can you tell me what this is?"

"That is a little red flower," said
Little Mouse.

"Look again," said Toad.
"It may look like a flower, but it isn't
a flower."

"That's silly!" laughed Little Mouse.
"See, I will pick it for you."

"Put me down!" cried a bug.
Little Mouse quickly dropped the bug
and ran.
Toad jumped along with Little Mouse.

Soon they came to a big tree.
"What is that on the ground?" asked Toad.

"There are leaves on the ground," said
Little Mouse, "and under the leaves
is a caterpillar."
He rushed to touch it.

"Look again," said Toad.
"It may look like a caterpillar, but it
isn't a caterpillar."

"Oh, my!" cried Little Mouse.
"It's a snake!"

"Can't I get a little sleep?" cried
the snake.
"Why did you wake me up?"
Little Mouse ran from the snake, and Toad
jumped along with him.

"Tell me," said Toad when they came
to a stop.
"What is it you can feel, but can't see?"

Little Mouse thought and thought.
"I don't know," he said.

"It is the wind," said Toad.
"You can feel it on your face, but you
can't see it."
Little Mouse sat down and laughed.

"Look again," said Toad.
"That is not a rock you just sat on."

"Get off my back!" cried a turtle.
"Why don't you go find a rock to sit on!"
Little Mouse jumped up.

"As I said," laughed Toad, "not all
things are what they look like."

Now the sun was on its way down in the sky.
Toad looked at the sun, and then at
Little Mouse.
"Night will come to the woods soon,
Little Mouse," he said.
"Go back to your home now, and do not go
outside at night."

"Why not?" asked Little Mouse.

"I just thought of a dream I had last night," Toad said.

"In my dream, the stars fell from their home in the sky.

Now do as I tell you!

Go home quickly!

Go home and hide!"

Then Toad rushed off to tell his friends.

Little Mouse ran home and hid.

Outside, he could hear Toad tell the animals of his dream.

"All of you, go home!" cried Toad.
"Stay there and hide!
The stars will fall from their home in
the sky this very night!"

Nobody wanted stars to fall on them,
so they did what Toad said.
The animals all ran home.
Soon the sun went down.
The woods were very still.

From his snug home Little Mouse looked up.
He could see the stars come out in the
night sky.

"They are very pretty," thought Little Mouse.
"I will just step outside to get a better look."

When he got outside, Little Mouse looked up at the pretty sky.

Then he looked down at the lake.

"There are stars in the water!" said Little Mouse.

"Toad was right.

The stars did fall from the sky.

They fell into the lake, and I am the only one to see them."

Little Mouse jumped up and down.

"All of you, come outside!" he called, but nobody came.

"Toad, Toad!" he called.

73

At last Toad rushed up.

"I hear you, Little Mouse," he said.

"I will save you!"

"You do not have to save me, Toad,"
said Little Mouse.

"The stars won't fall on us.
They are in the lake."

Toad looked.

"Oh!" he cried, and he rushed down to
the lake.

He jumped into the water.

"I touched the stars!" he cried.

But when he looked, there was only mud.

"Toad, you were right," laughed
Little Mouse.

"Not all things are what they look like!"

Thinking and Writing About the Selection

1. What was the little red flower?

2. Why do things trick Little Mouse again and again?

3. Toad says that you can feel the wind but not see it. Name two more things that you can feel but not see.

The River Is a Piece of Sky

From the top of a bridge
The river below
Is a piece of sky—
      Until you throw
      A penny in
      Or a cockleshell
      Or a pebble or two
      Or a bicycle bell
      Or a cobblestone
      Or a fat man's cane—
And then you can see
It's a river again.

The difference you'll see
When you drop your penny:
The river has splashes.
The sky hasn't any.

John Ciardi

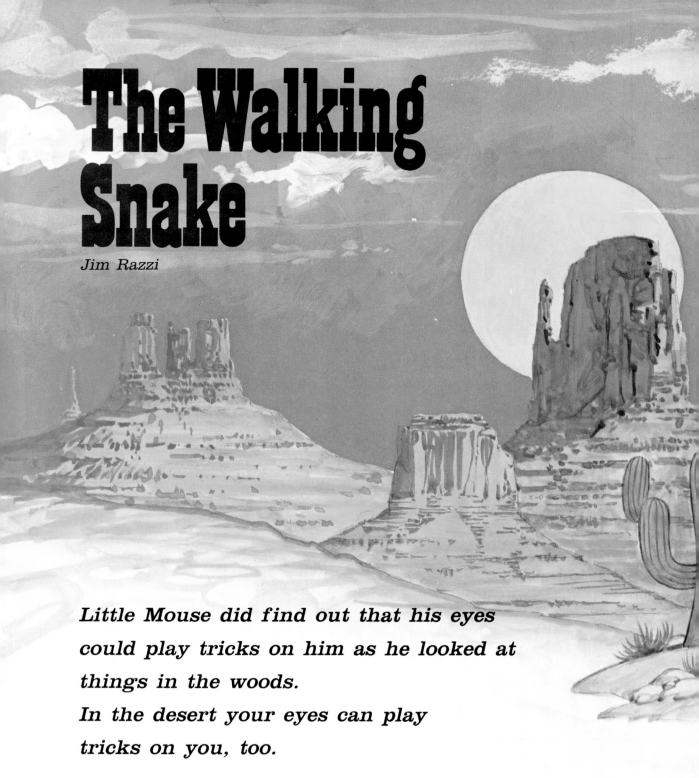

The Walking Snake

Jim Razzi

Little Mouse did find out that his eyes could play tricks on him as he looked at things in the woods.

In the desert your eyes can play tricks on you, too.

Tom's mother and father wanted to write a
book on the desert.
Tom went with them to look at the plants
and animals of the desert.
"How can I help?" asked Tom.

"Just write down all that you see and
hear, as we do," said his mother.

"I want to see a snake," said Tom.
"I will look for a snake to put in
your book."

"It feels like rain," said Tom's mother.
"Look, you can see it coming."
Tom looked up at the sky.
He could see the rain coming, and he
could *hear* it coming, too!

"We can go under that wide rock," said
Tom's mother, "so we won't get wet."
The rain fell just as the family
got under the rock.

Tom heard the rain as it fell on the rock.
He was happy that he was not wet.
"Dad, how will I know where to find a
snake?" he asked.

"You can tell where a snake was by
looking at its tracks," said Tom's father.
"Look at this book, Tom.
This is a book of animal tracks.
These are snake tracks.
You can look for tracks like these.
Then, if you are very quiet, you may see
the snake that made the tracks."

Tom looked at the book.
Soon he heard the rain stop.

"Wasn't that quick!" laughed Tom's mother
as the sun came out again.

"Now I can look for snake tracks!" said Tom.

82

Tom looked down at the desert floor, and
so did his mother and father.
His mother looked at a big cactus.
His father looked for little
desert animals.
Tom looked for snake tracks.

Then Tom called out, "Dad, Mother!
Come and see this!"
There were tracks by a cactus.
Were these snake tracks?
They looked a little like snake tracks,
but it looked as if the snake
were walking!
A walking snake?
"I never heard of a walking snake,"
thought Tom, "but you never know in
the desert!"
He looked for his mother and father,
but he did not see them.
"Dad said I have to stay very quiet if I
want to see the snake," he thought.

Tom went where the tracks led.
Then he looked up.
The tracks led to a desert home!

"What is this?" he said.

"Could a snake live in a home like this?"
The tracks led to the back of the
desert home.

"I want to see what made these tracks!"
said Tom.

He ran to the back of the home where the
tracks led, and there was what had made
the tracks!

It wasn't a walking snake at all!
It was a man, and Mother and Dad were
with him!
"Here is Tom!" said Mother.

Tom went up to the man.
"I thought, from looking at your tracks,
that you were a walking snake, but now I
can see how you made tracks like that!"
he said, laughing.

The man laughed and said, "I needed a log
for my home.
I can see why you thought my tracks
looked like a walking snake."

Mother and Dad laughed at the thought of a walking snake, too, but Tom laughed the loudest of all.
He was glad that the tracks had led to a laughing man and not to a walking snake!

Thinking and Writing About the Selection

1. Why is Tom's family in the desert?

2. What did they do when the rain came?

3. What is the walking snake?

SKILLS activity

MAIN IDEA

A paragraph is made up of sentences.
The sentences tell about the same thing.

Each sentence below says something about the pond.

> I like to go to the pond.
> I can swim at the pond.
> I watch the boats at the pond.
> I dig holes in the sand at the pond.

1. What sentence in the paragraph tells what all of the other sentences are about? Write the sentence on your paper.

> I like to go to the pond.
> I can swim at the pond.

I like to go to the pond.

Each sentence tells about food.

Use your senses when you try new food.

Look at the color of the food.

Smell and touch the food.

Then taste the food.

2. What sentence tells about the others?

Smell and touch the food.

Use your senses when you try new food.

Each sentence tells about the desert.

Plants and animals live in the desert.

Snakes live in the desert.

Cactus plants grow in the desert.

Some people live in the desert.

3. What sentence tells about the others?

Plants and animals live in the desert.

Cactus plants live in the desert.

ANIMAL TRACKS

Loretta Kaim

Tom wanted to look for snake tracks in
the desert.
You may have looked for animal tracks
by your home.
Have you seen them on the ground or in
the snow?
Could you tell what animal made
the tracks?

Animal tracks are like a map.
If you know how to read the signs, you can tell
all kinds of things.

You can tell what animal made the tracks.
What animal do you think made these tracks?

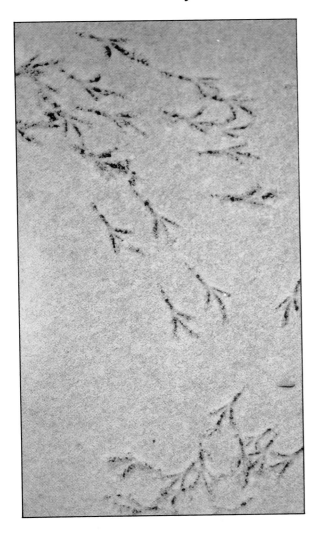

You can tell where the
animal went.
Where do you think
this squirrel went?

These tracks were made by a dog.
You can see the claws of a dog
in its tracks.

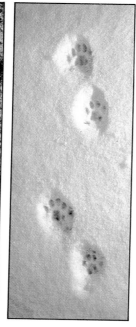

Cat tracks look like dog
tracks, but cats
keep their claws in when
they walk.
So you can't see the claws
of a cat in its tracks.

Doesn't it look as if the cat had
only two feet?
A cat will put its back feet into
the same tracks that the front
feet made.
The back feet go right where
the front feet were.

Now we will look at a rabbit's tracks.
A rabbit's front feet are little.
A rabbit's back feet are big.

When a rabbit hops, its back feet come
down in front, and its front feet come
down in back.
So if you see a rabbit's tracks, the back
feet will be in front!

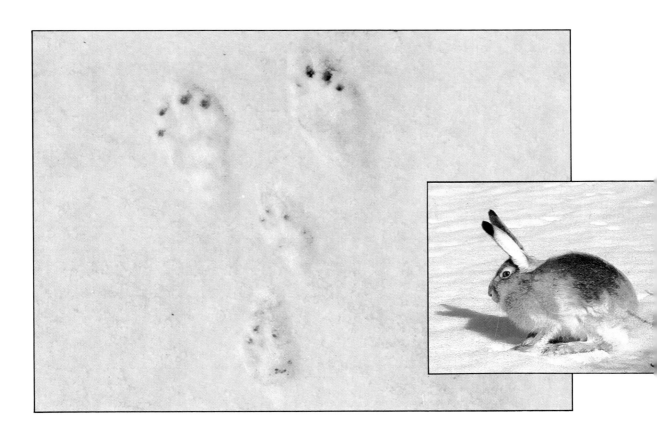

Not all animals make tracks with their feet.
Snakes don't have feet, so they make another kind
of track.
Some snakes make tracks that look like this.

Some snakes make
tracks that look
like this.

People make tracks, too.
The tracks people make are
called footprints.
When people put things on their
feet, their footprints do not look
the same.
What did these people have on?

Next time you go outside, see what
kinds of tracks you can find.
Look for tracks by your home or in a park.
Look for tracks on the ground or in the snow.

If you can be as quiet as a mouse and
not be seen, you may find the animal
that made the tracks.

Thinking and Writing About the Selection

1. How are cat tracks like dog tracks?

2. How are cat tracks not like dog tracks?

3. Write about more kinds of tracks you can
   find and the things that these tracks
   can tell you.

SKILLS activity

CONTEXT CLUES

Read each story below.
Think about the meaning of the
underlined word.
Write the sentence with the word
meaning on your paper.

There is a tiger at the zoo.
It looks like a cat.
The tiger has a long tail.

1. A tiger is _____.
   an animal
   a desert plant
   a bug

   A tiger is an animal.

A pond is full of water.
Fish live in a pond.
You can swim in a pond.

2. A <u>pond</u> is like ⎯⎯⎯⎯.
    a plant
    a lake
    a secret

Animals eat <u>food</u>.
People eat <u>food</u> every day.
You can cook <u>food</u> before you eat it.

3. <u>Food</u> is ⎯⎯⎯⎯.
    something animals and people eat
    a way to find things
    something you tell someone

Sara <u>whispered</u> in Sam's ear.
She didn't want her sister to hear.
She <u>whispered</u> a secret.

4. Something that is whispered is said ⎯⎯⎯⎯.
    in a quiet way
    in a loud way
    in a silly way

The Three Billy Goats Gruff

Retold by Margaret H. Lippert   Illustrated by Tim Hildabrandt

Some animals are so quiet, you have to see
their tracks to know where they went.
Some animals are not quiet at all.
Read "The Three Billy Goats Gruff"
and find out how a troll with very good ears
can hear every step these billy goats take.

Every day, the three Billy Goats Gruff
went out to eat grass.

They could eat the good green grass next
to their home.

Then they could walk down to the water
and eat the grass there.

There was a bridge over the water, but
they did not cross over it because a huge
troll had his home under it.

Then one day there was no more good grass
next to their home, and there was no more
down by the water.
They wanted good grass to eat.
"If we could cross the bridge we could
eat the good green grass over there,"
said the big billy goat.

"I will go first," said the brave little
billy goat.
"I am light, so the troll may not
hear me."
The little billy goat walked on
the bridge.
Trip, trap. Trip, trap.

But the troll did hear him.

"I hear someone," said the troll.

"WHO'S GOING OVER MY BRIDGE?"

"It is only I, the little Billy
Goat Gruff."

"I AM COMING TO EAT YOU UP!"
said the troll.

The little billy goat thought quickly.
"Do not eat me, for I am very little,"
he said.
"In a little while another billy goat
will come.
He is not as little as I am.
He will be better to eat."
The troll was happy to hear that,
and he let the little billy goat go on
over the bridge.

Then the next billy goat walked on
the bridge.

Trip, trap. Trip, trap.

"WHO'S THAT GOING OVER MY BRIDGE?"
said the troll.

"It is I, the next Billy Goat Gruff."

"I AM COMING TO EAT YOU UP!" said the troll.

"Don't eat me," said the billy goat.
"Let me go on over the bridge.
Wait for the last billy goat, who is
coming in a little while.
He is very big."
So the troll let that billy goat cross
the bridge, too, because he wanted to eat
the big billy goat.

Now the last billy goat walked on the bridge.
TRIP, TRAP. TRIP, TRAP.

"I hear someone big," said the troll.
"WHO'S THAT GOING OVER MY BRIDGE?"
"It is I, the BIG Billy Goat Gruff."

"At last you have come!" said the troll.
"I AM GOING TO EAT YOU UP!"

"Come and eat me if you can," laughed the
big billy goat.

Suddenly a huge head with big red eyes
came out from under the bridge.

"I AM COMING TO GET YOU!" said
the troll.

The big billy goat looked at the troll
and said, "You don't scare me."
Suddenly he put his head down and
rushed right at the troll.
He pushed the troll into the water.

Then the big billy goat went on over the
bridge to eat the new green grass.

"The troll will never scare us again,"
he said to his family.

"Now we can cross the bridge every day.
Here is all the good green grass
we can eat.

Now you can grow big and fat."

From that time on, the three Billy Goats
Gruff went over the bridge every day.

They all did grow big and fat on the good green grass.

The troll was never heard from again.

Thinking and Writing About the Selection

1. Why did the three Billy Goats Gruff want to cross the bridge?

2. Who went over the bridge first, and why?

3. How did the billy goats trick the troll?

Feeling Good

In this unit, you read about the five senses and how they help us learn.

You saw that the senses can trick us, too, as with Tom's walking snake, or Little Mouse and his stars in the mud.

You know much of what you do because you see, hear, taste, smell, and touch.

Thinking and Writing About *Feeling Good*

1. In "A Food Sale" why do Lupita and Charito make tacos?

2. What sense tricks the animals in "The Secret" when they play a game?

3. What did the troll hear over his home in "The Three Billy Goats Gruff"?

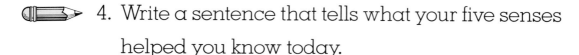 4. Write a sentence that tells what your five senses helped you know today.

Introducing Level 5

HELPING OUT

Friends are always glad to help each other out. In this unit, you will read about friends and families who help one another in many ways. What are some ways you could help your friends and family? How could they help you?

Because we do
All things together
All things improve,
Even weather.

Paul Engle

A DAY WITH GRANDMA AND GRANDPA

Carol Carrick

Talo likes to go and see Grandma
and Grandpa.
This time Talo will stay all night.
Read to see what Talo will dream.

Talo went to stay with Grandma and
Grandpa while his mother and father went
on a trip to the city.

Leo, the dog, played a game with Talo.
Talo would hide a hat, and then he would
say, "Go get your hat, Leo!"
Leo would go and find the hat.

When Talo went for a ride, Leo ran
next to him.
Grandma laughed and said, "Anything Talo
does Leo would like to do!"

Then Grandpa and Talo made a kite that
looked like a red bird.
"We can take it to the park," said Grandpa.

When Talo ran with the kite, it went way
up in the sky.
The wind blew it all over the lake.
Suddenly the tail came off, and down the
kite went, into the water.
"We should have made a fish kite," said Grandpa.

Grandma and Grandpa let Talo stay up late.
It was fun to sit outside and look at
the stars.
"Leo is tired," said Grandma.
"He had a big day.
You should be tired, too, Talo.
Come and help me fix your bed."

Grandma read to Talo, and then it was
time to go to sleep.
He had an aquarium for a night light.
He could lie there and watch the fish.
"I would love to swim like that,"
thought Talo.
"It would be fun to be a fish."

At last Talo slept, but he had a dream.
In his dream, a troll made Talo into a
frog, and a big snake wanted to eat
him up.
"Please don't eat me!" he wanted to say,
but not a word would come out.
All he could do was get a fly with
his tongue.

Talo got out of his bed to find Grandpa
and Grandma.
Grandpa was still in his chair outside.
"I can't sleep," cried Talo.
"I had a dream that I was a frog."

"I know how to fix that," said Grandpa,
and he picked Talo up and sat him on
his lap.
Grandpa rocked Talo in his chair.

"When I was just a boy," said Grandpa,
"I went to sea.
I wanted to sail and sail and see new
people and new things.
At night on the boat, I would lie in bed
and think of my family.
At first I cried, just a little.
You have to be brave on a boat.
But soon I slept.
The water rocked me to sleep."

"I love you, Grandpa," said Talo.

They rocked and rocked.

Soon Grandma came out to look for them.

"Are you all right?" she asked.

"Don't wake Grandpa," whispered Talo.

"I think he is having a good dream."

Thinking and Writing About the Selection

1. Where did the kite go?

2. What did Talo dream?

3. How does Grandpa make Talo feel better?

KEEP A POEM IN YOUR POCKET

Keep a poem in your pocket
and a picture in your head
and you'll never feel lonely
at night when you're in bed.

The little poem will sing to you
and the little picture bring to you
a dozen dreams to dance to you
at night when you're in bed.

So—
Keep a picture in your pocket
and a poem in your head
and you'll never feel lonely
at night when you're in bed.

Beatrice Schenk de Regniers

123

THIS IS HOW I HELP

Anne Rockwell

Grandpa and Talo helped one another.

It can be fun to be a helper.

How can you help people in your family?

How can you help your friends?

Read to see how one girl helps.

My mother says I am a good helper.

My father says so, too.

One time I helped my father make a kite.

I put the glue on the wood.

Then I helped my father fly the kite!

I help my mother, too.

One time she was doing her work, and Sue cried.

Sue is just a baby.

I played with her, and she laughed and laughed.

"I have just a little more work to do,"

said my mother.

"How would you like to feed the baby for me?"

I helped Sue eat and drink.

Then she was tired, and she went to sleep.

I love to help my mother bake.
I put in the water and then I mix.
It smells good when we bake.
It tastes good, too.

Oliver is my neighbor.
He comes to help when we bake.
He likes to stay and help eat what we bake, too.
"What a good helper you are!" says my mother.
"Now we can all clean up."

I can help Oliver, too.

He is not good at finding things, and I am very good at finding things.

"Can you help me find my mouse?" he asked me one time.

I did, because I like to help.

I help my mother and father clean the house.
I pick up my boat, my book, and my
animals, and put them in my room.
Then I make my room look neat.

We have five plants growing
in the sun.
I water them all, and no water
gets on the floor.
I water my little green cactus
and the plants with leaves
and flowers.
I water the new plants we are
growing for the neighbor.

129

I can help outside the house, too.
It is fun to help clean the car.
The dog would like to help us,
but it doesn't like the water.

I love to sit on the big rock and
wait for the woman with the mail.
I see the bus go by, and I see
a dog run by my house.
At last the woman comes with
the mail.
I can read the names on the mail.
I help when I go and get the mail.

Sue can't help at all, because she is too little.
"It is good that we have a big girl to
help us," my mother and father say.
They are right.
When my mother and father are tired, they
need a big girl to help them.
I am their big girl.

Thinking and Writing About the Selection

1. How does this girl help with the baby?

2. How does she help in the house?

3. How do you help at home?

WRITING activity

STORY

Prewrite

"This Is How I Help" is a story where photographs help tell the story along with sentences.

If the photographs were not there, the story would not make as much sense.

You can write a story like that.

You can have photographs in your story or draw your own pictures for it.

You need to make a plan for your story.

First , think of an idea.

Pick one of these or one of your own.

> My Family Trip
>
> What I Do Every Day
>
> My House

Next, plan the pictures for your story and the things you will say.

> What will come first?
>
> What comes next?
>
> What will come last in your story?

Write

1. Look at the plan for your story.

2. Draw pictures or pick photographs to go along with the things you wanted to say.

3. Next, write sentences for your story. Your first sentence should tell the idea you picked to write on.

4. Now, write one or two sentences to go under every picture or photograph.

Revise

1. Read your story. Have a friend read it , too.

2. Think of these things as you read. Do your sentences go with the pictures to make sense? Can you think of anything more you need to say in your story? Do you need to change the pictures or the sentences to make a better story?

My Mama Needs Me

Mildred Pitts Walter   *Illustrated by Pat Cummings*

Jason's mother just had a baby.
Jason does know that his mother
needs him, but he doesn't quite know
what he can do for her.
What can Jason do for his mother
and his new baby sister? Read and see.

Jason's friends rushed to his house
to see the new baby.
"Sh-h-h, she's sleeping," Jason said.

"Want to come play?" his friend asked.

"Can't," said Jason.
"The baby is home."

"So?" his friends said.

"So my mama needs me," said Jason.

135

Jason rushed into the house.

"Can I hold her?" he asked his mama.

"Not now.

When she wakes up," his mama said.

His father went back to work.

His mama went to bed.

Jason watched the baby.

She slept and slept and slept.

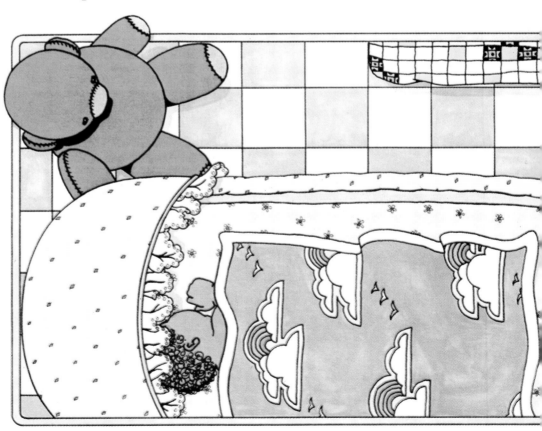

Jason went outside and sat on the
back steps.
He heard the hum of the city.
He heard his friends playing.
But there was only quiet in
his house.
"Nobody needs me," he thought.
"I need something to do!"

Soon Jason's mama got up.

Jason went back into the house.

"Are we going to make dinner?" he asked.

"Not now.

I want to sleep a little more,"

said his mama.

"Was she that tired when I was born?"

Jason thought.

He went outside.

Just then, Mr. Pompey, a neighbor, came along.

He was on his way to feed ducks at the pond.

"Hi, Jason," said Mr. Pompey.

"Want to come feed the ducks?"

Jason thought of the quiet house.

Then he thought of the baby.

"She won't wake up," he thought.

Jason went to his mama's room.

"Ma!" he whispered.

"You want me to do something?"

"Just let me sleep, Jason," said his mama.

"May I go with Mr. Pompey to feed
the ducks?" he asked.

"Yes, Jason," she said.

Jason and Mr. Pompey walked to the pond.

The ducks came up to Jason.

Mr. Pompey gave him a bag of bread.

Suddenly Jason thought, "What if my
little sister wakes up?"

He quickly handed the bread to Mr. Pompey.

"Feed the bread to the ducks," Mr. Pompey said.

"I can't," said Jason.

"I have to go.

My mama needs me."

When he got home, Jason waited.
There was still nothing but quiet.
"Why does she sleep so much?" he thought.
"I should have stayed at the pond."

At last his mama said, "Jason,
Jason, where are you?"

"Coming, Mama," he said, and
rushed into the house.

"You can help me now," his mama said.

"It is time for the baby to have a bath."

Jason helped his mama.

They gave the baby a bath.

Then Jason helped to pat her dry.

"Can I hold her now?" he asked.

"If you sit down," his mama said.

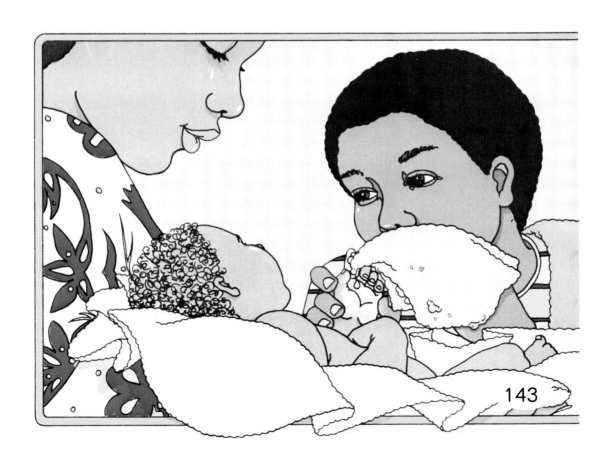

Jason sat with his little sister
on his lap.
All too soon she was sleeping again.
"You are a good helper," his mama said.
"But why don't you go and find
your friends?"

"Because," said Jason, "you need me.
Don't you need me?"

"Yes, I need you," said his mama.
"I need a big hug from you right now.
I love you, but that doesn't mean
you can't go play with your friends."

Jason gave his mama a big hug.
"That's what I needed to do," he thought.
He was so happy he gave her another hug.
Then he went out to play with his friends.

Thinking and Writing About the Selection

1. Why does Jason's mother need him?

2. Why doesn't Jason stay with Mr. Pompey and feed the ducks?

3. Why does Jason want to help so much?

Little

I am the sister of him
And he is my brother.
He is too little for us
To talk to each other.

So every morning I show him
My doll and my book;
But every morning he still is
Too little to look.

Dorothy Aldis

SKILLS activity

ANTONYMS

A. Look at the word with
a line under it in each sentence.

The girl is <u>dry</u>.   The girl is <u>wet</u>.

The words <u>wet</u> and <u>dry</u> are **opposites**.

Find the word in a box that is the
opposite of each word below.
Write the two words on your paper.

sad	up	big	yes	out	back

1. happy   <u>sad</u>   2. front   _____
3. no   _____   4. in   _____
5. down   _____   6. little   _____

148

B. Look at the underlined word in
each sentence.
Find the word in the box that is
the opposite.
Write the sentences on your paper.

day	wet	stop	kind	out

1. The rabbit was <u>dry</u> in his home.
   The rabbit got _____ in the rain.

2. The troll was <u>mean</u> to the goat.
   The farmer was _____ to the goat.

3. We can't see tracks at <u>night</u>.
   We will look for tracks the next _____.

4. The milk was <u>in</u> the bag.
   Mama took the milk _____ of the bag.

5. When the light is green, you <u>go</u>.
   When the light is red, you _____.

ANIMAL FAMILIES

Marlyn Mangus

*You know that people in a
family help one another.
Do animals live in families?
Do they help one another?
Read and find out.*

You live in a family.
Some animals live in
families, too.
Baby animals live with
their mothers and fathers in
animal families.
Baby animals sleep, eat, grow,
and change.
Their mothers and fathers
watch them and teach them.
Like you, animals play games.
Playing helps animals grow
up and learn how to get
along with one another.

Baby beavers are called kits.
Kits stay with their mothers in
the house when they are
very little.

Beavers are water animals, but
kits do not have to learn to swim.
They know how to swim as soon
as they are born.

When there is something the
matter, father beavers slap
the ground.
The kits run and dive into
the pond.

Baby beavers live with their fathers
and mothers for two years.

Mother bears teach their cubs to look for food.
Their sense of smell helps bears find the things
they like to eat.

Bears like fish, and they like leaves, too.
Trees are good places to find food.
Cubs learn that trees are good places to
hide, too.

Bear cubs stay with their mothers for two
years while they are growing up.

153

Baby lions are called
cubs, too.
The cubs live with
their fathers and
mothers in big families.

Lions sleep in the day.
They look for food
at night.
The cubs watch and
learn how to find food.
They learn to
run quickly.
They like to play.
They take three to
five years to
grow up.

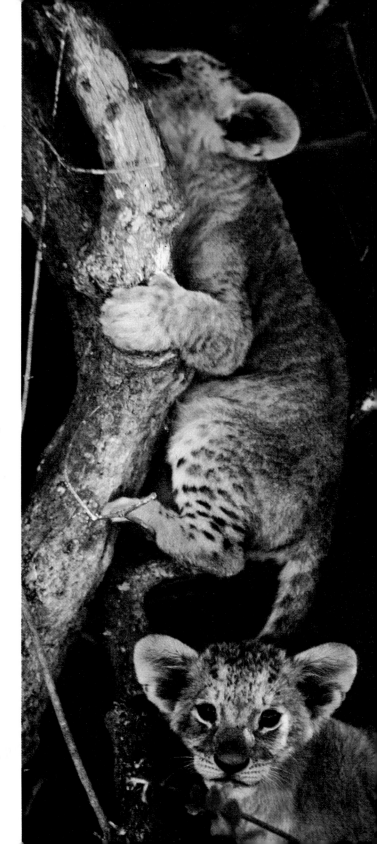

155

Elephant mothers and baby
elephants live in big families.
Baby elephants are called calves.

Elephants are huge animals.
Some calves are as big as people.
Why do you think elephants eat
much of the time?

Elephants teach their calves where
the plants they like to eat grow.
They show them where to
find water.

Elephant calves learn by watching and doing.
They may hold the tail of their mother for help.

Elephants like to play in the water.
They like to take a mud bath, too.

An elephant is a baby for quite a while.
Calves stay with their mothers for 12 to 15 years
while they are growing up.

Now you know how some animals live in families.
In their families, animals grow and learn from
one another.

Thinking and Writing About the Selection

1. What do father beavers do when something
   is the matter?
2. What kinds of things do animal mothers and
   fathers teach their families?

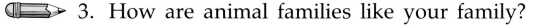 3. How are animal families like your family?

SKILLS activity

STORY TITLE

A story should have a title.
The title should tell the big idea of the story.
Read each story below.
Then pick a name for each story.
Write the name you picked on your paper.

1. Amanda looks for animal tracks.
   She looks near the pond.
   She looks in the woods.
   At last she finds tracks near a dog house.

   A good name for this is _____.
   Animal Tracks
   A Dog House for Amanda
   In the Woods

2. Babies sleep most of the time.
   They sleep at night and in the day.
   Sometimes they wake up to eat.
   Sometimes they wake up to cry.

158

A good name for this is _____.

What Babies Do

Babies Always Eat

Babies Always Sleep

3. Beavers are water animals.

They live near ponds.

Beavers know how to swim when they are born.

They like to swim at night.

A good name for this is _____.

Beavers and Water

Beavers Swim at Night

Baby Beavers Can Swim

4. Baby animals have their own names.

Baby beavers are called kits.

Baby bears are called cubs.

Baby lions are called cubs, too.

Baby elephants are called calves.

A good name for this is _____.

Bears and Lions

Beavers Are Kits

Baby Animals

THE SOUP STONE

Retold by Margaret H. Lippert

People may not know how they can
help one another.
They may not think they have anything
to give.
Can you make something from nothing?
Read and see.

One day a man was on his way home
from a trip.

He was walking along thinking of food.

The sun was going down, and he was tired.

"It is late," he thought.

"I won't get home in time for dinner."

Just then he saw a woman outside
a big house.

"I am in luck," he thought.

"I will ask her for something to eat."

When he got to the house, he asked the
woman for some food.

"I do not have anything to give you," she said, going into the house.

The man thought quickly.
Then he picked up a stone.
"I have a surprise for you," he called to the woman.
"All I need is some water.
With some water, I can make good soup from a stone."

"Soup from a stone?" said the woman.
"I never heard of that.
How do you make it?"

The man showed her the stone.
"This is a soup stone," he said.
"First you need to put some water into a big pot.

Then you drop in the soup stone. When the water gets hot, you will have stone soup."

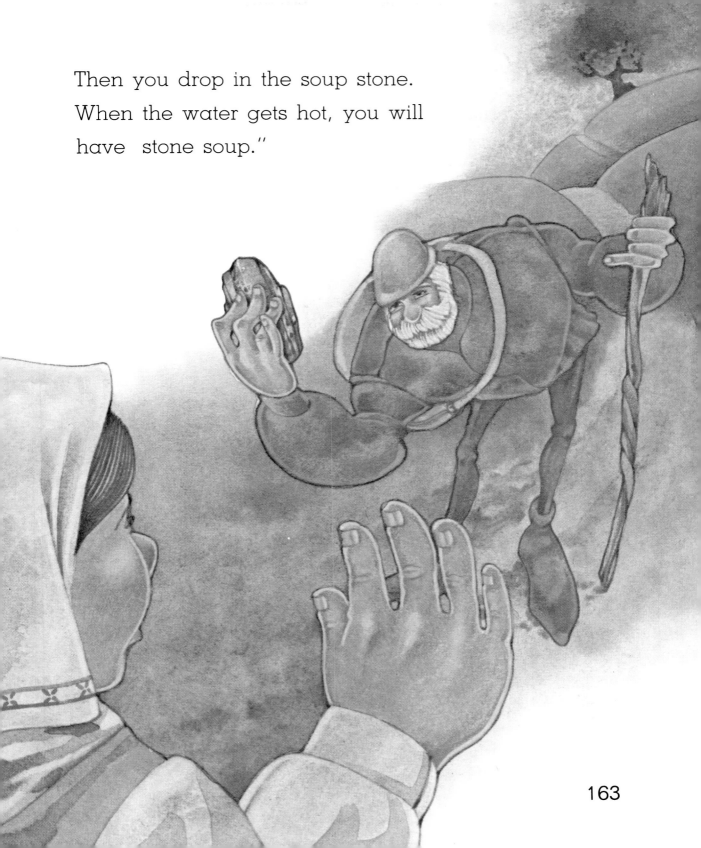

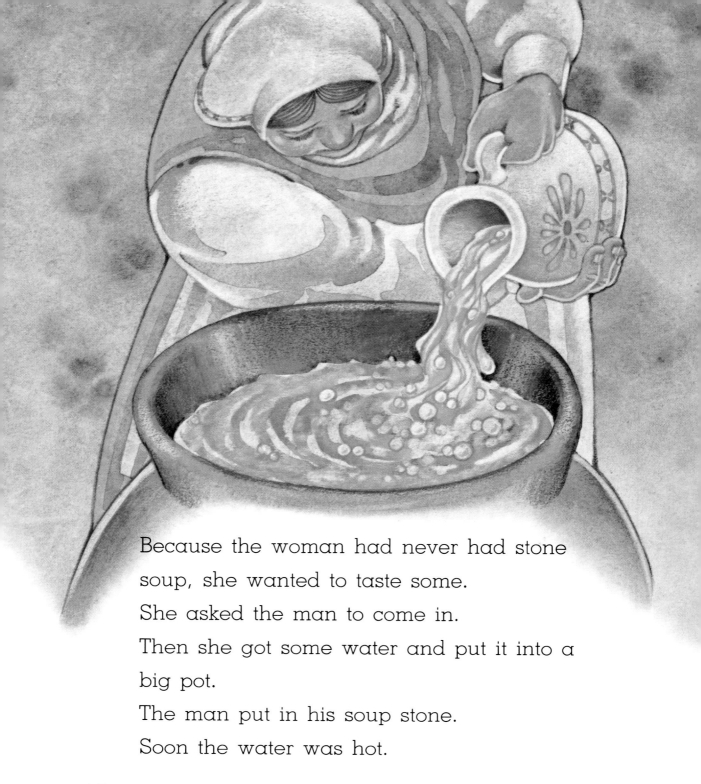

Because the woman had never had stone
soup, she wanted to taste some.
She asked the man to come in.
Then she got some water and put it into a
big pot.
The man put in his soup stone.
Soon the water was hot.

"Now I will taste the soup," said the man.
The man ate a little soup.
"This soup is good, but some carrots
would make it better," he said.

"I think I could find some carrots," the
woman said.
She got some carrots and gave them to
the man.
He put them into the pot.

A boy came in.

"I smell something good," he said
to his mother.

"What you smell is stone soup,"
said his mother.

"May I taste some?" asked the boy.
The boy ate a little soup.
"This soup is good," he said, "but some
potatoes would make it better."
The boy went out to get some potatoes.

As the boy was coming back with the potatoes, his sister saw him.

"What are we having for dinner?" she asked.

"We are having stone soup," he said.

"Stone soup?" she asked.

"Yes," he said.
"It is good.
Come in and taste it."
The girl went in with the boy.

The boy put the potatoes into the pot, and the girl ate a little soup.
"This soup is good, but some chicken would make it better yet," she said.
"I will get some chicken."
The girl got some chicken and put it into the pot.

In a little while, the man said, "We can eat now."

"Please go and get your father," the woman said to the boy.
The boy went out to get his father.

When the father came in, he said, "Something smells good.
What is it?"

"It is stone soup," said the woman.

"All we need now is some bread to eat with the soup," said the father, and he got some bread.

The family sat down to eat.
"Please sit down," the woman said
to the man.
"You showed us how to make stone soup.
Now I would like you to have dinner
with us."
The man sat down.

When they all had soup and bread in front
of them, the woman looked into the pot.
"There is too much soup in here for us to
eat," she said.
"The neighbors may want some.
I will go and ask them."

The woman called to her neighbors.
"Come in," she said.
"Have some of this good stone soup."

They ate all they could hold.
"This soup was a surprise," the woman
said to the man.
"Thank you for a good dinner."

"A good soup stone makes good soup,"
said the man.
"If you like, I will give you this one."

"Thank you," said the woman.
"Now I can make stone soup!"

Thinking and Writing About the Selection

1. Who made the stone soup?

2. What was in the stone soup?

3. How does the woman change?

The Rabbit Food Summer

Gibbs Davis

How do you make a new friend?

Mona would like to be friends with Luz,

but she does not quite know how to do it.

Read and see what Mona will do.

172

Luz spoke to the tree.
"Every summer it's the same.
All my friends go on a trip with their
families and leave me with nobody
to play with."
She went out onto a long branch.
She could see the school roof
and playground.
She saw the roof of a friend, and
she began to feel sad.

173

Suddenly the tree began to shake.

Luz looked down to see Mona.

All Luz's school friends made fun of Mona.

"Just my luck," she whispered.

"Want to play?" asked Mona.

Luz wanted to shout, "Don't bother me!"
but her mother would hear.

Luz's mother said she should try to be
kind because Mona didn't have a friend,
but Luz didn't want to.
"Why are you so big?" she asked.

"Baby fat," said Mona.
"But I won't be fat for long.
I am going to eat nothing but
rabbit food all summer."

Luz jumped down onto
the ground.
"What is rabbit food?"
she asked.

"I am finding some for my dinner,"
said Mona.
"Want to come?"

"I will tag along," said Luz.
She didn't have anything better to do.
Mona led her onto the playground
by the school.
Luz thought of her friends on the school
ball team when she saw the playground.
She began to feel sad again.

Mona looked down at the ground.

She handed Luz a bag.

"Please open this bag for me," she said.

Then she began to drop leaves, grass,
and bugs into the open bag!

"A rabbit likes to eat bugs," she said,
and she began one of her songs—

"Pick a rabbit out of a hat, eat a bug so
you won't get fat.

Carrots, flowers, grass, and leaves, I eat
bugs like they grow on trees!"

Luz began to hum along.

Mona *was* fun to be with.

She picked up some grass and said, "If you like rabbit food, try this."

She pushed the grass in Mona's face.

"Don't bother to look.

Just open wide!" she said.

Mona looked at the grass in Luz's hand
for a long time.
When she saw a bug in with the grass, she
looked as if she would cry.
"I can't," she whispered.
"The only rabbit food I eat is carrots.
I can't eat bugs and grass.
I made that up.
I just wanted to be your friend."

"You don't *have* to eat bugs to be my
friend," said Luz.
"I like to make up games, too.
Want to come over to my house for dinner?"

Mona looked happy.
"What are you having?" she asked.

"Chicken," laughed Luz, and she made a
rabbit face.
"Chicken with carrots!"

Thinking and Writing About the Selection

1. Why is Luz sad at first?

2. How did Luz feel when she saw Mona?

3. Why does Mona say that she is going to eat nothing but rabbit food all summer?

SKILLS activity

CAUSE OF AN EVENT

Read the sentences below.

He made soup $\boxed{\text{because}}$ there was no food.

She likes carrots, $\boxed{\text{so}}$ she put them in the soup.

Sometimes one thing will cause another thing to happen.

Look at the words in the boxes.

These words help tell you why something happened.

Read the sentences.

Then write the answer to the question.

1. The boy wanted a taste because the soup
   smelled good. The soup was hot.

Why did the boy want a taste of soup?
   The soup was hot.
   The boy was tired.
   The soup smelled good.

2. There was too much soup, so the woman
   gave some to her neighbors.
   They ate all they could.

Why did the woman give some soup to her neighbors?
   The soup was cold.
   They had helped make the soup.
   There was too much soup.

3. The soup was good because everyone had
   put something in it. It was more than
   water and a stone.

Why was the soup good?
   Everyone had put something in it.
   It had a stone in it.
   The soup was made of water.

184

Who's in Rabbit's House?

Adapted by Verna Aardema   Illustrated by Leo and Diane Dillon

Someone is in Rabbit's house.

Rabbit would like one of her big friends to help her.

She doesn't think that a little frog can help.

Read and see who will help Rabbit.

PLAYERS:

STORYTELLER	LONG ONE	FROG
GIRLS	RABBIT	LEOPARD
BOYS	RHINOCEROS	ELEPHANT

STORYTELLER: Every day the animals of the woods
went to the lake to drink.
They went by Rabbit's house.
Rabbit sat outside her house and
watched them.
One day Rabbit had a big surprise.
She could not get into her house!
She banged on the door.
She heard a big voice.

LONG ONE: I am the Long One.
I eat trees and trample on elephants.
Go away, or I will trample on you!

186

RABBIT:	That's my house! Come out now!
STORYTELLER:	**She banged on the door again.**
GIRLS:	*Ban, ban, ban!*
LONG ONE:	Go away!

STORYTELLER:	**Frog was watching.**
	She went up to Rabbit.
FROG:	I think I could get him out.
RABBIT:	You are so little.
	You think you could do
	what I can't?
	Go away!
STORYTELLER:	**Frog hid by a tree.**
	Along came Leopard.

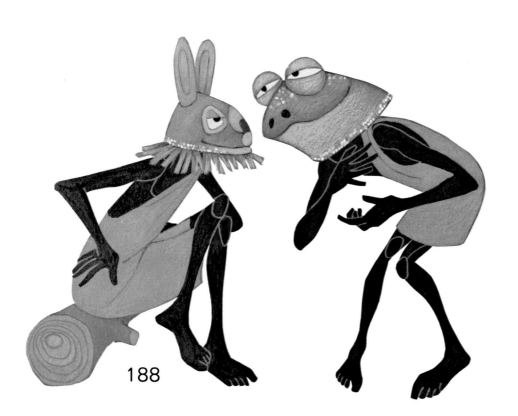

188

RABBIT: Leopard, someone is in my house.
He won't come out, and I can't get in.

LEOPARD: Who's in Rabbit's house?

LONG ONE: I am the Long One.
I eat trees and trample on elephants.
Go away, or I will trample on you!

LEOPARD: You don't scare me!

189

STORYTELLER: Leopard jumped onto the little
                house and began to scratch.
                Bits of roof went this way and that.

BOYS: *Zzp, zzp, zzp.*

RABBIT: Stop!
                My house won't have a roof!
                Go away!

STORYTELLER: Leopard went down to the lake.

GIRLS: *Pa, pa, pa.*

STORYTELLER:	**Rabbit went up onto her roof.**
	She began to fix it.
	Along came Elephant.
ELEPHANT:	What are you doing, Rabbit?
	Does your roof leak?
RABBIT:	Someone is in my house.
	Leopard wanted to scratch it to bits.
	Now I have to fix my roof.
ELEPHANT:	Who's in Rabbit's house?
LONG ONE:	I am the Long One.
	I eat trees and trample on elephants.
	Go away, or I will trample on you!
ELEPHANT:	Trample on elephants?
	Who thinks he tramples on elephants?
	I will trample you flat!
	Flat as a mat!
	I will trample you, house and all!

STORYTELLER: **Elephant went toward the little house.**

BOYS: *Gumm, gumm, gumm.*

RABBIT: Stop!
Don't trample on my house!
Go away!

STORYTELLER: **Elephant went down to the lake.**

GIRLS: *Gumm, gumm, gumm.*

STORYTELLER: **Along came Rhinoceros.**

RABBIT: Rhinoceros, someone is in my house!

RHINOCEROS: Who's in Rabbit's house?

LONG ONE: I am the Long One.
I eat trees and trample on elephants.
Go away, or I will trample on you!

RHINOCEROS: I will toss you into the lake,
house and all!

STORYTELLER: **Rhinoceros put his head down and
went toward the little house.
Rabbit jumped onto his nose.
Rhinoceros tossed his head.
Up and away went Rabbit, and into
the lake.**

BOYS: *Glish!*

RHINOCEROS: That's it for the Long One.

FROG: But that was Rabbit you tossed into
the lake!

STORYTELLER:	**Elephant saw Rabbit in the lake. She walked in and saved Rabbit.**
ELEPHANT:	I saved you, Rabbit, but you are a bother!
RABBIT:	Thank you, Elephant!
STORYTELLER:	**Rabbit went back to her house. She sat on a log and began to cry.**
RABBIT:	*Wolu, wolu, wolu.*
STORYTELLER:	**Frog went up to Rabbit.**
FROG:	Don't cry, Rabbit. I think I could get that bad animal out of your house. Please let me try.
RABBIT:	How?
STORYTELLER:	**Frog made a horn from a big leaf. When she spoke into it, it made her voice very loud.**
FROG:	Who's in Rabbit's house?

194

LONG ONE: I am the Long One.
I eat trees and trample on elephants.
Go away, or I will trample on you!

FROG: I am the spitting cobra!
Come out of that house, or I will come
under the door and spit poison at you!
SSSS!

195

STORYTELLER: The door opened.

GIRLS: *Hirrr.*

STORYTELLER: Out came a long, green caterpillar.
He was so scared, his legs jumped
this way and that.

RABBIT: It's only a caterpillar!

LONG ONE:	Don't let the spitting cobra get me! I was only playing a joke!
RABBIT:	Oh, Long One. The spitting cobra was only Frog!
STORYTELLER:	**Frog laughed and laughed.**
FROG:	*Gedung, gedung, gedung.*

Thinking and Writing About the Selection

1. Why did Rabbit not let Frog help her at first?

2. What did Leopard do to help Rabbit?

3. Who was the Long One?

Verna Aardema

Verna Aardema was one of nine children, so there was not much quiet reading time at home. Then she got an "A" on a poem written for school. Her mother realized that she could write well and encouraged her. Verna Aardema decided to be a writer.

She began writing stories for children when she had a little girl of her own. "She wouldn't eat without a story," Aardema recalls. So she made up stories for her. Now Aardema gets many of her book ideas from old African folktales. Then she changes them so that today's readers can understand them better. Verna Aardema loves to act out her stories. Try one yourself!

More to Read   *Behind the Back of the Mountain*
Why Mosquitoes Buzz in People's Ears

LANGUAGE ACTIVITY

SOUNDS ALL AROUND

Some words sound just like sounds. "Who's in Rabbit's House?" has words that sound like sounds. Look at the pictures of the animals. Read the words. Make the sounds that answer the questions.

Ban, ban, ban

Zzp, zzp, zzp

Gumm, gumm, gumm

Glish

Wolu, wolu, wolu

Gedung, gedung, gedung

1. What sound did Rabbit make when she cried?

2. What sound did Elephant's feet make?

3. What sound did Rabbit make when she banged on the door?

4. What sound did Leopard make on the roof?

5. What sound did Frog make when he laughed?

6. What sound did Rabbit make when she fell into the water?

What other "sound" words can you make up?

199

TEACH US, AMELIA BEDELIA

Peggy Parish   *Illustrated by Lynn Sweat*

The telephone was ringing.
"I'm coming, I'm coming,"
said Amelia Bedelia.

200

She answered the telephone.
"Mrs. Rogers!" she said.
"Where are you?"

"I'm at the airport in Pinewood," said
Mrs. Rogers.

"You didn't tell me you were going
away," said Amelia Bedelia.

"I'm not," said Mrs. Rogers.
"I'm meeting the new teacher.
But her plane is late."

"That's too bad," said Amelia Bedelia.

"The telephone at the school is out of
order," Mrs. Rogers went on.
"Please go to Mr. Carter's office
at the school.
Tell him what I said."

"I'll go right now," said Amelia Bedelia.

201

Amelia Bedelia got her things.

She walked to school.

"Where is Mr. Carter's office?" she asked.

"That first door," said a child.

Amelia Bedelia walked in.

"Mrs. Rogers tried to call you," she said.

"But your telephone is out of order."

"I know," said Mr. Carter.

"But thank goodness you're here.

The children are going wild.

Miss Lane left a list for today.

I'll take you to the room."

He handed Amelia Bedelia the list.

"Follow me," he said.

They went down the hall.

Mr. Carter opened a door.

Children were all over the place.

"All right," said Mr. Carter.

"Quiet! This is your new teacher."

"Me! Teach!" said Amelia Bedelia.

But Mr. Carter was gone.

She looked at the children.

They looked at her.

"I'm Amelia Bedelia," she said.

The children giggled.

"You're nice," said Amelia Bedelia.

"I do like happy children.

But we have a lot to do."

She held up the list.

"We must do just what this says,"

204   she said. "Now what's first?"

Amelia Bedelia read, "Reading time.
I know about that," she said.
"I read my cookbook.
It tells me just what to do."
She held up a book.
She said, "Is this the right one?"

"Yes," said Amanda.

Amelia Bedelia opened the book.
"I declare," she said.
"This is a good one.
Are you ready?"

"Yes," said the children.

"All right," said Amelia Bedelia.
"It says, 'Run, run, run.'"
The children just sat.

Amelia Bedelia clapped her hands.
"Run," she said. "Run, run, run."
Amelia Bedelia ran.

The children ran after her.

Around the room, through the halls,

around the block they ran.

Finally they ran back into the room.

Amelia Bedelia plopped on her chair.

"That takes care of run, run, run,"

she said.

"Your book plumb tired me out.

Let's see what's next.

I hope we don't have to run to do it."

She looked at the list.
"Here are some problems for you,"
she said.

"Yuck!" said the children.

"Ginny, get your apples,"
said Amelia Bedelia.

"What apples?" said Ginny.
Amelia Bedelia looked puzzled.
She said, "But it says
Ginny has four apples.
Paul takes away two.
Oops," said Amelia Bedelia.
"I don't think I was supposed
to tell that part."
She read the other problems.
"These all have apples in them," she said.
"Does anybody have apples?"
The children shook their heads.

Then Amelia Bedelia had an idea.
"Let's go to my house," she said.
"We have lots of apples."

"Yes!" shouted the children.

"We better leave a note,"
said Amelia Bedelia.
She went to the blackboard and wrote,

Then off they went
to the Rogers' backyard.

Amelia Bedelia got the apples.
She called some children.
"There is a problem for each of you,"
she said.

"You all have apples.

Somebody is going to try
to take some away.
Are you going to let them?"

"No!" shouted the children.

Amelia Bedelia went to the other children.
"You are supposed to take away some of
their apples," she said.
She told each child whom to take from.
"Can you do that?" she asked.

"Sure!" said the children.

209

"All right, everybody,"
said Amelia Bedelia. "Go!"
Children started after each other.
They ran all over the yard.

Amelia Bedelia turned and
went into the kitchen.
She put some of this and a lot of that
into a big pot.

She put the pot on the stove.

"There," she said.

"I'll surprise them."

Amelia Bedelia started out.

Just then Mr. Rogers started in.

"What is all of this?" said Mr. Rogers.

"What are those children doing?"

"Math," said Amelia Bedelia.

"Math!" said Mr. Rogers.

"Come see," said Amelia Bedelia.

They went out.

"That's not fair, Steve," yelled Janet.

"You hid your apples. I can't take any."

"That's not fair, Judy," shouted Andy.

"You took away all my apples."

"What in tarnation are they doing?"
said Mr. Rogers.

Amelia Bedelia read him the problems.

"That sounds like fun.

I'm going to help them," he said.

He joined the children.

"Now that does beat all," said Amelia Bedelia.

212   She went inside.

Later she called, "Everybody come.
All apples on the table."
Apples came from everywhere.
Amelia Bedelia put a stick in each one.
Then she dipped them in the pot.

"Taffy apples!" everybody shouted.

"Right," said Amelia Bedelia.
"Take one and go home. School is out."

The children grabbed apples.
They crowded around Amelia Bedelia.
"Please, please teach us again,"
each one said.

Amelia Bedelia said nothing.
She looked at her kitchen
and shook her head.
Mrs. Rogers walked in.
Someone was with her.

"What happened?" she said.
"Where are the children?"

"Home," said Amelia Bedelia.

"Home!" said Mrs. Rogers.
"But it's not time."

"It was for me," said Amelia Bedelia.

"This is Miss Reed," said Mrs. Rogers.
"She is the new teacher.
She came to get the children."

"Then she will have to find them,"
said Amelia Bedelia.
214 "I'm plumb tired out."

"But, but . . ." said Miss Reed.

"More taffy apples," called Mr. Rogers.

"Taffy apples!" said Mrs. Rogers.
"Come on, Miss Reed."
Amelia Bedelia put the taffy apples on
the table.
They all sat down and ate.

"I'll let you teach anytime," said Miss
Reed, "if you will make taffy apples."

"Be glad to," said Amelia Bedelia.
"I do love children."

215

Helping Out

In this unit, you read about families and friends who help one another.

You read about helping at home.

You read about helping friends when they need you.

Sometimes people want to help but do not know how.

Can you think of ways to help people?

Thinking and Writing About *Helping Out*

1. How do Grandpa in "A Day with Grandma and Grandpa" and Jason in "My Mama Needs Me" help someone?

2. In "Who's In Rabbit's House?" how does Frog save Rabbit?

3. How are animal families like people families?

4. Write a sentence that tells how you help your friends and family.

Picture Dictionary

A a

again
Tom has seen the show one time.
He wants to see it <u>again</u>.

along
The dog will go <u>along</u> with the boys to the woods.

as
Louise was <u>as</u> quiet <u>as</u> a mouse.

away
Jane is going <u>away</u> on a trip.

B b

baby
The <u>baby</u> can sit in a chair,
but she needs Mother to help her eat.

bath
Father and Jenny give
the baby a <u>bath</u>.

be
Mark will <u>be</u> in bed by eight o'clock.

B b

bears
<u>Bears</u> are big animals
with claws on their feet.

beavers
Do you see how <u>beavers</u>
can make a pond?

because
Tom ran quickly to school <u>because</u> he was late.

beef
Jeff and his father like <u>beef</u>.

began
When all the family had sat down
at the table, they <u>began</u> to eat.

blind
People who are <u>blind</u> can't see.

born
When a baby is <u>born</u>, it is
very little and can't do much.

B b

bother
Mother said not to <u>bother</u>
the baby when it is sleeping.

Braille
Blind people can learn to read <u>Braille</u>.

bread
"The <u>bread</u> smells good," said Tami.
"May I have some to eat?"

bridge
A <u>bridge</u> is a track or way over a pond or lake.
You can cross the water by walking on the <u>bridge</u>.

by
You can find out about animals <u>by</u> watching them.

C c

cactus
The <u>cactus</u> is one kind of plant
that can grow in the desert.

C c

called
Mother <u>called</u> Billy to come home.

calves
Baby elephants are called <u>calves</u>.
What other baby animals
are called <u>calves</u>?

carrots
<u>Carrots</u> are plants that we eat.

caterpillar
A <u>caterpillar</u> is a little bug that
looks like a snake with feet.

chicken
A <u>chicken</u> is a bird.

claws
Cats, dogs, and other kinds of animals
have <u>claws</u> on their feet.

coming
Oliver's friends are <u>coming</u> to his house.

D d

dinner
The family will eat chicken and potatoes for <u>dinner</u>.

door
Linda opened the <u>door</u>.

E e

ears
What will Kim put on her <u>ears</u>?

eat
What kinds of food do you like to <u>eat</u>?

elephant
An <u>elephant</u> is a huge animal with gray skin.

F f

families
Animals have <u>families</u> with mothers and fathers.

floor
Footprints on the <u>floor</u> make Mom mad.

F f

food
Fish, nuts, beef, and tacos are all <u>food</u>.

footprints
Amy and her father leave <u>footprints</u> in the snow.

from
The robin flew <u>from</u> the birdhouse to the tree.

front
Your face is the <u>front</u> of your head.

G g

give
Scott and Jerry <u>give</u> the animals their dinner.

grandma
Your <u>grandma</u> is the mother of your father or mother.

grandpa
Your <u>grandpa</u> is the father of your father or mother.

G g

gruff
If someone says a word in a <u>gruff</u> way,
he or she may scare you.

H h

happy
Sally is <u>happy</u> to see her friends.

having
We are <u>having</u> a flower show at school now.

head
Your <u>head</u> has a nose, two eyes, and two ears.

hear
Mother can <u>hear</u> the
girls laughing.

heard
Paco <u>heard</u> what Ann whispered to Pat.

helper
Mike is a good <u>helper</u> when
Mother makes dinner.

H h

her
Clara and <u>her</u> family live in Mexico.

here
"We can stop <u>here</u> in the park to eat," said Mother.

hi
Carlos sees his friend on the bus and says, "<u>Hi</u>!"

hold
Claws help a bird <u>hold</u> on to a branch.

horn
The man is playing a <u>horn</u>.

house
"I live in this <u>house</u>," said Jack.

I i

it's
Ted can't find his book. <u>It's</u> under the chair.

K k

kinds
There are two <u>kinds</u> of fish in the aquarium.

kits
Baby beavers are called <u>kits</u>.

L l

learn
Ted will <u>learn</u> how to skate by watching and doing.

leopard
A leopard is a kind of big cat.

love
Mother and Father <u>love</u> Charles and the baby.

M m

ma
When Dan comes home, he gives his mother a hug and says, "Hi, <u>Ma</u>! How are you?"

Mexico
José showed us <u>Mexico</u> on the map.

mother's
The little cat played with its <u>mother's</u> ear.

much
In winter, there may be <u>much</u> snow on the ground.

N n

neighbor
Leo's <u>neighbor</u> lives in the house next to his.

nobody
All the food is still here. <u>Nobody</u> wanted to eat it.

nose
Your <u>nose</u> is on your face.

O o

oh
"Oh, no!" cried Jane, as she dropped the glue.

only
Only one girl will win the game.

onto
The cats smell the fish
and jump onto the table.

open
Mother and Father open their mail.

or
"You may watch a show, or you
may read a book," said Father.

over
Mother and Father put
a rug over the floor.

P p

people
What are all the people
looking at?

P p

please
We say please when we want someone to help us.

poison
Poison is something that is bad. Never taste or eat it.

pond
We saw a frog jump into the pond.

potatoes
Potatoes grow in the ground.

Q q

quiet
Don't say a word and keep still. Be very quiet.

R r

rhinoceros
A rhinoceros is a big animal with a horn on its nose.

roof
The roof of the house is green.

R r

room
Kim has her own <u>room</u>, where she can work, play, and sleep.

rushed
Mark <u>rushed</u> to get to school on time.

S s

saw
Billy <u>saw</u> the watch in the grass and went to pick it up.

scare
"I know who you are.
You are Tim, and you don't <u>scare</u> me," said Joanne.

school
We learn to read and write in <u>school</u>.

scratch
Cats like to <u>scratch</u> with their claws.

secret
"It's our <u>secret</u>," said Jan. "Do not tell it to people."

senses

Our five senses let us see, hear,
feel, taste, and smell.

should

When you see a red light, you should stop.
You should wait for the green light and then go.

silly

The girls laughed when
Ned made a silly face.

sister

Tom is with his family.
His mother, his father, and his sister are in the car.

skin

A frog may have green skin.

slapped

Jack slapped the book down on the chair.

slept

Darlene slept while the sun came up.

S s

snug
Amanda is <u>snug</u> in her bed.

some
<u>Some</u> boats are green and
<u>some</u> boats are red.

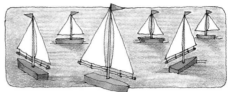

someone
The girls need <u>someone</u> to help them read the signs.

something
The cat sees <u>something</u> under the bed.

soon
"The bus should come <u>soon</u>," said Jason's mother,
as they waited at the bus stop.

soup
"We are having <u>soup</u>
for dinner," said Mother.

spit
A baby may <u>spit</u> out food
it doesn't like.

S s

spitting cobra
The spitting cobra is a snake
that can poison people.

stay
When Kate leaves,
the dog will stay home.

still
"If you keep quiet and stay very still,
the rabbit may come to you," said Father.

stone
A stone is a rock you can hold in your hand.

storyteller
What will the storyteller tell about this time?

suddenly
It suddenly started to rain.

surprise
Dad has a surprise
outside for Tami.

T t

tacos
Tacos are a food made with beef.

taste
Cats love the taste of fish.

teach
Kate can teach Tim
how to write his name.

thank
"Thank you for my new books, Grandma,"
said Ted, as he gave her a hug.

their
The girls wanted a pet of their own.

them
Nan has six cats.
She feeds them every day.

these
"These books on the
chair are mine," said Linda.

T t

think

First Sally will read the story,
then she will <u>think</u> about it.

three

There are <u>three</u> boats in the pond.

tiger

A <u>tiger</u> is a big animal
of <u>the</u> cat family.

tiger's

A <u>tiger's</u> coat helps hide the tiger.

tired

Jan and Cindy have had a long trip.
They are <u>tired</u> and want to go to sleep.

tongue

We taste with our <u>tongue</u>.

touch

Should Leo <u>touch</u> the cactus?

T t

toward
When Mother called Ned to come home,
he ran quickly <u>toward</u> the house.

trample
Elephants are so big
that they <u>trample</u> growing
things where they walk.

troll
A <u>troll</u> is someone in a story who may
be very small or may be a giant.

V v

voice
"We can't hear you," said Mr. Pompey.
"You will have to tell us in a loud <u>voice</u>."

W w

went
The boys <u>went</u> from the zoo to the aquarium.

W w

while
Ted and Jack read
while Mary and Jill play.

whispered
The boys whispered when they
were asked to be quiet.

why
Do you know why we have night and day?

won't
We won't play outside if it is raining.

work
Mona and Paco work with Father
to help make the house snug.

would
Jason would have walked home if it wasn't raining.

Y y

years
Father shows Jane how long two years is.

Word List

To the teacher: The following words are introduced in *Look Again!* The page number to the left of a word indicates where the word first appears in the selection.

Instructional-Vocabulary Words are printed in black. Words printed in red are Applied-Skills Words that children should be able to decode independently, using previously taught phonics skills. Story Words are printed in blue. These are proper names and content area words that children need to be familiar with to read a particular selection.

Unit 1
Feeling Good

My Five Senses
10. five
    senses
11. hear
    ears
    nose
    taste
    tongue
    skin
    touch
12. it's
    face
13. hears
15. sense
16. seeing
    feel

16. feels
    helps

The Pet Frog
18. stay
    her
19. floor
20. pond
    bugs
    silly
22. here
    soon
    plan
    why
24. tell
    frog's

The Secret
28. hug
    them
29. raining
    having
30. secret
    whispered
    ear
    as
    snug
    three
    rug
31. tiger
    tiger's
32. Mother's
33. slapped
    fell
34. top
    oh

237

Louise

38. blind
40. tricks
41. makes
    happy
    that's
42. she's
43. cane
    won't
44. school
    again
45. please
    still
    wait
    waited
46. Braille
48. touched

A Food Sale

50. food
    sale
51. trip
    Mexico
    along
52. because
    went
54. tacos

54. way
55. mix
    beef
56. eat
58. much
    tastes
    smells
    who's

**Look Again,
Little Mouse**

65. animals
    flower
66. Toad
67. caterpillar
    rushed
    snake

70. dream
    from
    their
    hid
71. nobody
73. called
74. save
    only
    mud

**The Walking
Snake**

80. rain
    coming
    wide
    wet
81. heard
    by
    these
    quiet
82. wasn't
    quick
83. cactus
84. led
86. laughing
    needed
    log
87. glad

Animal Tracks

90. or
91. kinds
    think
92. claws
    front
93. rabbit's
    be

This part of *Look Again!* is a review of
letters and the sounds they stand for.
Looking carefully at these letters
will help you know how to say and read
many new words.

Word Work Table of Contents

Lessons

1 Initial Consonants

A. Say each picture name. Listen for the beginning sound. Find the letter that makes the word that names the picture. Write each word on your paper.

b	c	d	h	l	m	s	r

1. ___all

2. ___og

3. ___ar

4. ___ome

5. ___un

6. ___oon

7. ___ion

8. ___ug

B. Look at each sentence.
Find one letter that can begin *all*
the words that need a first letter.
Then, write the sentences on your paper.
Remember to make the first letter of each
sentence a capital letter.

1. ___inda ___ikes ___ooking at
    ___eopards.

s	l	d	r

b	c	h	m

2. ___e ___id ___is ___at ___ere.

3. ___ud on the ___at ___akes ___y
    ___other ___ad.

m	b	s	h

r	l	b	s

4. ___am ___ang ___ix ___illy ___ongs.

5. The ___abbit ___ushed ___ight
    under a ___ock.

r	c	m	s

6. ___ad ___oesn't like ___ays in
    the ___esert.

m	h	d	b

7. He ___ame by ___ar with a ___at
    in his ___oat.

h	c	b	l

8. The wind blew the ___oat like
    a ___ig ___ird on water.

l	s	d	b

2 Final Consonants

A. Find the letters that make words that name each picture. Write the words on your paper.

| n | t | d | g | k | ck | l | ll | s | ss | m |

1.  the hea___ of a rhinocero___

2.  a squirre___ in the gra___

3. a ma___ with a ba___

4.  a boo___ and an aquariu___

5.  a cra___ in the clo___

6.  a ba___ and a ba___

B. Find the letters that make the words.
Write the sentences on your paper.
When you have written the sentences,
read them together as a rhyme.

n	t	d	l	s

1. Betty ha__ a little goa__.

2. He was so much fu__.

3. He liked to see the schoo__ bu__ come.

4. The__ home the two would ru__.

k	m	t

5. My fish is in an aquariu__.

6. It does not sing. It does not hu__.

7. What it does is swi__ all day.

8. Tha__ is its wor__, and tha__ is its play.

n	t	d	ll	ss	ck	g

9. A do__ and a ca__ cro__ the sea.

10. Their boa__ is gree__ and re__.

11. But soo__ they wi__ come ba__, you see.

12. For it's time to go to be__.

245

3 Short Vowels and Graphemic Bases

A. Look at the picture and read the three words. On your paper, write the word that names the picture.

1. fat   fan   far

2. bad   bet   bat

3. set   sad   sag

4. men   met   man

5. pat   pad   pet

6. bed   bag   bad

7. ban   bat   bag

8. fed   fat   fad

B. Find the word that fits in the sentence. Then write the sentence with the word in it.

1. This animal is my _____.   pet   pat

2. I like it better _____ a dog.   than   that

3. It is not a _____.   can   cat

4. It is a _____.   hen   hat

5. One day she _____ away!   ran   red

6. That made me feel _____.   sat   sad

7. I went to _____.   bad   bed

8. I could not sleep _____ night.   than   that

9. The next day, I _____ .   sat   sad

10. _____ I saw something.   Then   Than

11. The _____ of hen feed
    was moving!   beg   bag

12. I looked in, and there was my
    _____ hen!   fat   fan

4 Short Vowels and Graphemic Bases

A. Read the words in each box.
What is the same about the two words?

| s<u>it</u> | s<u>ock</u> | h<u>ug</u> |
| h<u>it</u> | cl<u>ock</u> | r<u>ug</u> |

The words in each box have the same ending sound.
They have the same vowel sound. The words *rhyme*.

Read each group of words in the box. Find two words
that rhyme. Write the two words on your paper.

1.
| him |
| his |
| hum |
| Tim |

2.
| pop |
| not |
| sit |
| hot |

3.
| rock |
| duck |
| luck |
| sick |

4.
| stop |
| hop |
| sip |
| lot |

5.
| tip |
| top |
| rip |
| hit |

6.
| lock |
| fix |
| box |
| fox |

7.
| bug |
| cup |
| mop |
| pup |

8.
| run |
| men |
| snug |
| fun |

B. Find the word that fits in the sentence.
Then write the sentence with the word in it.

1. Kim was _____.　　　　sun　　sick　　sock

2. This was no _____.　　　fox　　fun　　fit

3. Mom came in with a
   _____ of soup.　　　　cup　　cot　　cap

4. Kim had a _____.　　　　sit　　sum　　sip

5. Mom gave Kim a _____.　hop　　hug　　hot

6. Dad had a _____
   for Kim.　　　　　　　　box　　bit　　bop

7. In it was a _____.　　　cluck　clock　click

8. There was a leaf
   on _____.　　　　　　　tip　　top　　tock

9. The leaf was for
   good _____.　　　　　　lick　　lock　　luck

10. Kim asked Dad to
    _____ with her.　　　　sock　　six　　sit

249

5 Initial Consonant Clusters

A. Say the picture name. Find letters
to make the word that names the picture.
Write the word on your paper.

tr	gr	br	pl	sl	bl

1.  ___ee

2.  ___andpa

3.  ___idge

4.  ___andma

5.  ___ants

6.  ___eep

7. ___ed

8.  ___ock

9.  ___oll

10.  ___ead

250

B. Find the letters to make a
word that fits in the sentence.
Write the sentence on your paper.

tr	gr	br	pl	sl	bl

1. In summer, I take a __ip.
2. I go to see my __andpa.
3. I like to __eep at his house.
4. Grandpa has a big __ee.
5. In summer, it is __een.
6. We __ant flowers by it.
7. The flowers __oom all summer.
8. Grandpa and I __ay games by the tree.
9. We eat __ead and soup there.
10. Then we walk to the __idge.
11. We __y to get big fish.
12. I __an to be with Grandpa every summer.

6 Long Vowels and Graphemic Bases

A. Say the picture name. Find letters that name the word. Write the word on your paper.

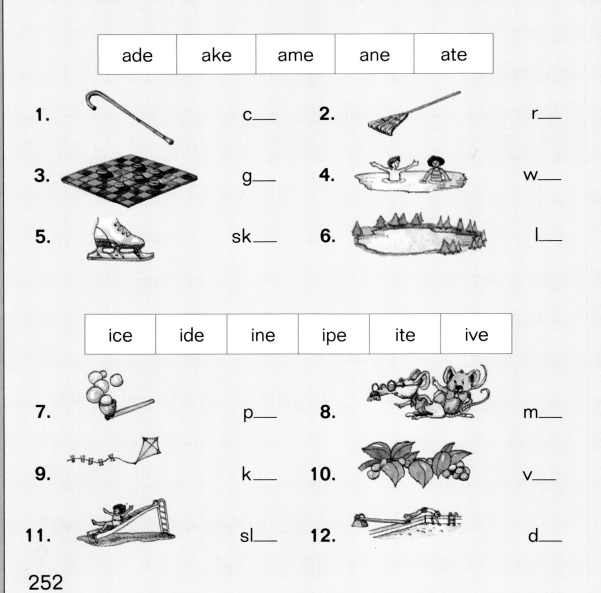

ade	ake	ame	ane	ate

1. c___ 2. r___

3. g___ 4. w___

5. sk___ 6. l___

ice	ide	ine	ipe	ite	ive

7. p___ 8. m___

9. k___ 10. v___

11. sl___ 12. d___

B. Read the sentence.

Write it on your paper.

Underline two or three words that rhyme.

1. Beef with rice is very nice.
2. Don't take a rake to the lake.
3. What is the name of this game?
4. There are nine in my line.
5. Why is your skate out by the gate?
6. Ten of us can swim and five can dive.
7. We saw a bride ride down the slide.
8. Can we wipe the pipe dry?
9. I will trade the birdhouse I made.
10. That is quite a nice kite.

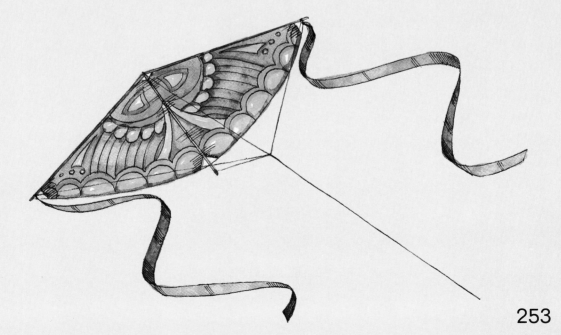

7 Long Vowels and Graphemic Bases

A. Read each word in the box.
Do you hear the long vowel sound?
Look at the letters that stand for
the long vowel sound.

sp**o**k**e**	m**u**l**e**	n**ee**d
b**o**n**e**	h**u**g**e**	f**ee**d

Read each sentence. Find the word with
the long o, the long u, or the long e sound.
Write the word on your paper.

1. Has John seen Tom's bug?

2. It's a cute little thing.

3. It has six feet.

4. Tom fed it seeds.

5. But Tom feels sad.

6. Does Tom hope his bug will run back?

7. Tom thinks a robin stole it.

8. Is it under a stone?

9. Is this just a joke?

B. Read the sentences.
Make a word to finish the sentences.
Write the word on your paper.

oke	ole	one	uge	eed	eet

1. A ground squirrel is an animal.
   It lives under the ground.
   It lives in a h___.

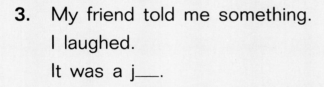

2. My pet is very, very big.
   It is h___!

3. My friend told me something.
   I laughed.
   It was a j___.

4. I walk on these.
   They are my f___.

5. A dog would like this.
   It is a b___.

6. A bird likes to eat this.
   It is a s___.